Marketing Magic

Chapter 1: The Marketing Playground

Welcome to the exciting world of marketing! Just like a playground, marketing is full of different tools and strategies to help your business thrive. In this chapter, we'll take a stroll through the marketing playground and explore the basics of what makes a business stand out.

Imagine marketing as a giant puzzle, and each piece represents a way to connect with your audience. From colorful social media posts to eye-catching ads, every piece plays a crucial role in creating a complete picture of your brand.

Chapter 2: Know Your Audience

In the magical land of marketing, understanding your audience is like discovering a treasure map. Who are your customers? What are their interests, needs, and desires? By unraveling these mysteries, you'll be able to tailor your marketing efforts to captivate their hearts and minds.

We'll uncover the secrets of creating customer personas – imaginary characters that represent your ideal customers. Get ready to embark on a quest to discover what makes your audience tick!

Chapter 3: Spells of Storytelling

Every great wizard has a captivating story, and so should your business! In this chapter, we'll delve into the art of storytelling and learn how to weave spells that enchant your audience.

From the humble beginnings of your business to the challenges you've overcome, your story adds a magical touch that sets you apart from the rest. Get ready to sprinkle a bit of fairy dust on your brand and watch your customers fall under the spell of your narrative.

Chapter 4: Social Media Sorcery

Ah, social media – the enchanting realm where businesses and customers connect in the blink of an eye! In this chapter, we'll unravel the secrets of social media sorcery and explore how to cast spells that make your brand shine.

From creating engaging posts to mastering the art of hashtags, you'll become a social media wizard in no time. Get ready to take your business on a journey through the magical world of likes, shares, and retweets.

Chapter 5: Potion Crafting – The Art of Content Marketing

Just like a skilled potion maker, content marketing involves mixing the right ingredients to create a concoction that delights your audience. In this chapter, we'll explore the magic behind blogs, videos, and infographics.

Learn the ancient art of SEO (Search Engine Optimization) and discover how to brew potions that make your business appear on the first page of search results. Get ready to become a content wizard and concoct potions that leave a lasting impression.

Epilogue: Your Marketing Adventure Continues

Congratulations, brave marketer! You've completed the first chapters of your magical marketing adventure. But remember, the journey never truly ends. With new spells and strategies emerging, your marketing magic will continue to evolve.

May your brand flourish, your audience grow, and your marketing spells continue to captivate the hearts of customers far and wide. Happy marketing, and may the magic be with you!

Chapter 6: The Alchemy of Email Enchantment

Ah, the mystical world of email! Like an alchemist turning base metals into gold, email marketing has the power to transform casual readers into loyal customers. In this chapter, *we'll uncover the secrets of crafting spellbinding emails that captivate your audience.*

Learn the art of creating compelling subject lines that lure readers into opening your emails. Discover the magic of personalized content that speaks directly to the hearts of your subscribers. Get ready to master the alchemy of email marketing and turn your email campaigns into enchanting spells.

Chapter 7: Enchanted Analytics – Unveiling the Magic Numbers

In the enchanted forest of marketing, analytics are the magical compass guiding you on your journey. In this chapter, we'll delve into the world of key performance indicators (KPIs) and metrics that reveal the effectiveness of your spells.

Learn how to interpret the magic numbers – from website traffic to conversion rates. Uncover the secrets of A/B testing to refine your strategies and make your marketing spells even more potent. Get ready to wield the power of analytics and steer your marketing journey in the right direction.

Chapter 8: Community Conjuring – Building Magical Connections

In the kingdom of marketing, building a community is like creating a magical haven for

your brand. In this chapter, we'll explore the art of community building and how it can elevate your business to new heights.

Discover the magic of engaging with your audience on social media and forums. Learn how to respond to comments and reviews, turning customers into brand advocates. Get ready to weave a sense of belonging and create a community that becomes a powerful ally in your marketing adventures.

Chapter 9: The Quest for Influencers

In the vast landscapes of marketing, influencers are the knights and sorcerers who can amplify your brand's message. In this chapter, we'll embark on a quest to find and collaborate with influencers who can cast spells of endorsement on your business.

Learn the art of identifying influencers in your niche and building meaningful partnerships. Explore the benefits of influencer marketing and how it can expand the reach of your brand. Get ready to join forces with influencers and watch your marketing magic reach new realms.

Chapter 10: The Ever-Evolving Magic

As you conclude this magical journey through the realms of marketing, remember that the magic never truly ends. In this final chapter, we'll explore how staying adaptable and embracing new trends keeps your marketing spells fresh and effective.

Discover emerging trends like augmented reality, voice search, and sustainability in marketing. Learn the importance of continuous learning and staying attuned to the evolving preferences of your audience. Get ready to embark on a lifelong quest for marketing mastery, where the magic is ever-changing and always enchanting.

Epilogue: The Legacy of Marketing Magic

Congratulations, master marketer! You've completed your initiation into the world of marketing magic. As you continue your journey, remember that the legacy of your marketing spells will live on in the hearts and minds of your audience. May your brand continue to flourish, and may your marketing magic leave an indelible mark on the world. Happy spellcasting!

Chapter 11: The Enchanting World of Video Marketing

Enter the mesmerizing realm of video marketing, where moving images and storytelling converge to create powerful spells. In this chapter, we'll explore the magic of videos and how they can elevate your brand's narrative.

Learn the art of creating engaging video content, from captivating product demonstrations to behind-the-scenes glimpses of your business. Discover the wonders of live streaming and interactive videos that invite your audience to be part of the magic. Get ready to wield the enchanting powers of video marketing and captivate your audience in a whole new dimension.

Chapter 12: Mobile Sorcery – Crafting Spells for Small Screens

In the enchanted forest of marketing, mobile devices are the magic wands that connect you with your audience on the go. In this chapter, we'll delve into the world of mobile marketing and how to cast spells that resonate with users on small screens.

Explore the art of responsive design and create mobile-friendly content that ensures a seamless experience for your audience. Uncover the secrets of mobile advertising and harness the magic of location-based marketing. Get ready to enchant users in the palm of their hands and make your brand an integral part of their mobile journey.

Chapter 13: Navigating the Social Media Maze

The social media maze is a labyrinth of opportunities waiting to be explored. In this chapter, we'll embark on a quest through the various platforms and discover how to navigate the twists and turns of social media marketing.

Learn the nuances of each platform – from the visual allure of Instagram to the conversational magic of Twitter. Uncover the secrets of paid advertising on social media and how to create viral content that spreads like wildfire. Get ready to navigate the social media maze with finesse and cast spells that resonate across different platforms.

Chapter 14: Mindful Marketing – Crafting Ethical Spells

In the enchanted kingdom of marketing, ethical considerations are the guiding principles that shape your spells. In this chapter, we'll explore the importance of mindful marketing and how to craft spells that resonate with integrity and authenticity.

Discover the magic of purpose-driven marketing and how aligning your brand with social and environmental causes can create a positive impact. Learn how transparency and honesty can build trust with your audience. Get ready to infuse your marketing spells with mindfulness and create a legacy of ethical enchantment.

Chapter 15: The Future of Marketing Magic

As we gaze into the crystal ball of the future, the possibilities for marketing magic are boundless. In this chapter, we'll explore emerging technologies and trends that will shape the future of marketing.

From artificial intelligence and virtual reality to the integration of voice-activated devices, the future holds exciting possibilities. Learn how to stay ahead of the curve and adapt your marketing spells to the ever-changing landscape. Get ready to embrace the future of marketing magic and continue your journey as a master spellcaster in the dynamic world of business.

Epilogue: A Never-Ending Tale of Marketing Magic

Congratulations, marketing maestro! You've traversed through the enchanted lands of marketing magic, mastering spells that have woven the story of your brand. As you bid farewell to this book, remember that the tale of marketing magic is a never-ending one. May your spells continue to dazzle, captivate, and leave an enduring legacy in the hearts of your audience. Happy spellbinding!

Chapter 16: The Evolution of AI in Marketing

In this chapter, we'll explore the ever-expanding role of artificial intelligence (AI) in shaping the future of marketing. Dive into the world of chatbots, personalized recommendations, and predictive analytics that AI brings to the table. Learn how businesses are leveraging AI to understand customer behavior, automate tasks, and enhance the overall customer experience. Through case studies, witness firsthand the transformative power of AI in modern marketing.

Chapter 17: The Rise of Influencer Culture

As we navigate the ever-changing landscape of marketing, influencers continue to play a pivotal role in shaping consumer preferences. Uncover the latest trends in influencer marketing, from micro-influencers to nano-influencers. Explore successful case studies that highlight how brands are collaborating with influencers to create authentic connections with their target audience. Learn the art of finding the right influencers for your brand and crafting compelling partnerships that resonate.

Chapter 18: Interactive and Immersive Content

Step into the world of interactive and immersive content, where engagement is king. From augmented reality (AR) experiences to virtual reality (VR) campaigns, discover how brands are breaking through the noise with innovative and captivating content. Explore case studies that showcase the impact of interactive content on user engagement and brand loyalty. Learn how to incorporate these technologies into your marketing arsenal and create memorable experiences for your audience.

Chapter 19: Data Privacy and Ethical Marketing

In an era where data privacy is paramount, ethical marketing practices are gaining prominence. Explore the latest trends in data privacy regulations and how businesses are adapting their marketing strategies to build trust with consumers. Delve into case studies that exemplify ethical marketing approaches, demonstrating transparency, consent, and responsible data usage. Learn how prioritizing privacy can be a competitive advantage and a key driver of customer loyalty.

Chapter 20: Omnichannel Experiences and Seamless Integration

As consumer touchpoints multiply, providing a seamless omnichannel experience is crucial for success. Dive into the world of omnichannel marketing, where the integration of online and offline channels creates a cohesive brand journey. Explore case studies of brands that have mastered omnichannel marketing, delivering consistent messaging and experiences across various platforms. Learn how to leverage technology and data to create a unified customer experience that spans physical and digital realms.

Epilogue: The Continuous Journey of Marketing Mastery

Congratulations, marketing virtuoso! As you conclude this comprehensive guide, remember that the journey of marketing mastery is continuous. Stay vigilant to the evolving trends, embrace emerging technologies, and remain adaptable to the changing preferences of your audience. Explore real-time case studies, attend industry conferences, and engage with the marketing community to stay at the forefront of the magical world of marketing. May your marketing spells continue to enchant, captivate, and leave an indelible mark on the ever-evolving landscape of business. Happy marketing !

Chapter 21: Practical Tips for Implementing AI in Marketing

Now that we've explored the impact of artificial intelligence (AI) in marketing, let's delve into practical tips for its implementation. Learn how to integrate chatbots into your website, automate personalized email campaigns using AI algorithms, and leverage predictive analytics for targeted advertising. This chapter provides step-by-step guides on selecting AI tools, training your team, and measuring the success of AI-driven marketing strategies.

Chapter 22: Navigating the Influencer Marketing Landscape

Embarking on an influencer marketing journey? This chapter offers practical tips for finding the right influencers, negotiating collaborations, and measuring the ROI of your influencer campaigns. Follow a step-by-step guide on identifying influencers aligned with your brand values, drafting effective collaboration agreements, and utilizing influencer marketing platforms to streamline the process.

Chapter 23: Creating Interactive and Immersive Content

Ready to captivate your audience with interactive and immersive content? This chapter provides actionable tips for incorporating augmented reality (AR) and virtual reality (VR) into your marketing strategy. Follow step-by-step guides on creating AR experiences for mobile devices, developing VR campaigns, and measuring user engagement. Learn how to make these technologies accessible to your audience with easy-to-follow implementation guides.

Chapter 24: Ensuring Data Privacy and Ethical Marketing Practices

Maintaining data privacy and adhering to ethical marketing practices is essential. This chapter offers practical tips for ensuring compliance with data protection regulations, gaining user consent, and building trust with your audience. Follow step-by-step guides on creating transparent privacy policies, implementing secure data storage practices, and conducting ethical marketing campaigns. Learn how to turn data privacy into a competitive advantage with actionable implementation tips.

Chapter 25: Crafting Seamless Omnichannel Experiences

Creating a seamless omnichannel experience requires careful planning and execution. This chapter provides practical tips for aligning your online and offline channels, ensuring consistent messaging, and delivering a unified brand experience. Follow step-by-step guides on implementing omnichannel technologies, leveraging customer data for personalization, and measuring the effectiveness of your omnichannel strategy. Learn how to use technology to bridge the gap between physical and digital touchpoints with actionable implementation advice.

Epilogue: Your Practical Guide to Marketing Mastery

Congratulations on completing this comprehensive guide to marketing mastery! As you embark on implementing these strategies, remember that practical tips and step-by-step guides are your allies. Stay updated on the latest trends, continuously assess your strategy, and adapt to the evolving landscape. Engage with industry experts, attend workshops, and seek mentorship to enhance your practical marketing skills. Your journey to mastery is ongoing, and with these actionable insights, may your marketing endeavors continue to enchant, captivate, and leave a lasting impact on your audience. Happy marketing!

Chapter 26: Mastering Social Media Strategies

Social media has become an integral part of every marketer's toolkit. In this chapter, we'll delve into practical social media strategies for success. From content creation to community engagement, these tips will empower you to harness the full potential of social platforms.

26.1 Content is King: Crafting Compelling Posts

The foundation of social media success lies in compelling content. Learn how to create visually appealing and engaging posts tailored to each platform. This chapter provides step-by-step guides on designing eye-catching graphics, writing impactful captions, and incorporating multimedia elements to boost your social media presence.

26.2 The Art of Consistency: Establishing Posting Schedules

Consistency is key in the world of social media. Discover practical tips for establishing posting schedules that align with your audience's online behavior. Follow step-by-step guides on utilizing scheduling tools, analyzing optimal posting times, and maintaining a consistent brand voice across different platforms.

26.3 Building a Community: Fostering Engagement

Social media is not just a broadcast channel; it's a community hub. This chapter explores strategies for fostering engagement, building relationships, and turning followers into brand advocates. Learn how to respond to comments, run interactive polls, and host live sessions to create a sense of community around your brand.

26.4 Data-Driven Decisions: Analyzing Social Media Metrics

To refine your social media strategy, it's crucial to analyze metrics and insights. Follow step-by-step guides on interpreting key performance indicators (KPIs), such as engagement rates, click-through rates, and conversion metrics. Discover how to use analytics tools to make informed decisions and optimize your social media campaigns for success.

26.5 Paid Advertising Mastery: Boosting Reach and Conversions

While organic reach is valuable, paid advertising can amplify your impact. Explore practical tips for creating effective social media ads, targeting specific demographics, and optimizing ad budgets. This chapter provides step-by-step guides on setting up ad campaigns, A/B testing, and analyzing the ROI of your paid social efforts.

26.6 Staying Trendy: Navigating Social Media Trends

Social media trends evolve rapidly, and staying ahead is vital for success. Learn how to identify and leverage current trends, from utilizing new features on platforms to participating in viral challenges. This chapter offers practical tips on incorporating trending topics into your content strategy and maintaining relevance in the dynamic social media landscape.

26.7 Influencer Collaborations: Partnering for Impact

Influencer collaborations can significantly expand your reach. Explore practical strategies for identifying and partnering with influencers aligned with your brand. Follow step-by-step guides on establishing effective collaborations, measuring the impact of influencer marketing, and maximizing the benefits of these partnerships for your brand.

26.8 Crisis Management: Navigating Challenges Effectively

In the digital age, crises can unfold on social media. Learn how to navigate challenges, respond to negative comments, and turn crises into opportunities for positive brand engagement. This chapter provides practical tips and step-by-step guides on developing a crisis management plan, monitoring online conversations, and maintaining a resilient social media presence.

Epilogue: Your Social Media Success Journey

As you conclude this chapter on social media strategies, remember that success is an ongoing journey. Embrace the dynamic nature of social media, stay adaptable to emerging trends, and continuously refine your strategies based on real-time insights. Engage with your audience authentically, experiment with different approaches, and measure your success through tangible metrics. Your mastery of social media will empower your brand to thrive in the interconnected digital landscape. Happy socializing!

Chapter 27: Harnessing the Power of User-Generated Content

User-generated content (UGC) has become a force to be reckoned with in the realm of social media. In this chapter, we'll explore how to harness the power of your community to create authentic and impactful content.

27.1 Encouraging User Participation: Creating Contests and Challenges

Encourage your audience to become content creators by organizing contests and challenges. Learn how to design engaging prompts, set clear guidelines, and promote participation. This chapter provides step-by-step guides on leveraging user-generated content to increase brand visibility and foster a sense of community.

27.2 Curating User Stories: Showcasing Real Experiences

Your customers' stories are powerful tools for building trust. Discover practical tips for curating and showcasing user stories on your social media channels. Follow step-by-step guides on collecting testimonials, creating customer spotlight features, and using real experiences to humanize your brand.

27.3 Establishing UGC Campaigns: Mobilizing Your Audience

Create strategic campaigns to mobilize your audience and generate user content around specific themes or products. Learn how to initiate and run UGC campaigns effectively, including setting objectives, creating branded hashtags, and incentivizing participation. This chapter offers practical tips and guides for maximizing the impact of UGC campaigns.

27.4 Incorporating UGC into Marketing Collateral

User-generated content can be seamlessly integrated into your broader marketing collateral. Explore strategies for incorporating UGC into your website, email campaigns, and even traditional advertising. Follow step-by-step guides on obtaining permissions, maintaining brand consistency, and amplifying the reach of user-generated content beyond social media.

27.5 Leveraging Instagram Stories and Reels for UGC

Instagram Stories and Reels provide dynamic platforms for user-generated content. Dive into practical tips for encouraging your audience to share their experiences through these features. This chapter offers step-by-step guides on creating interactive elements, leveraging stickers and polls, and maximizing the visibility of user-generated content on Instagram.

27.6 Turning Customers into Advocates: UGC as a Trust-Building Tool

Transform your satisfied customers into brand advocates through UGC. Learn how to build relationships with your audience, encourage authentic content creation, and leverage the influence of satisfied customers. This chapter provides practical tips on turning user-generated content into a trust-building tool that resonates with your wider audience.

27.7 Monitoring and Moderating UGC: Maintaining Quality and Brand Alignment

While UGC can be a powerful asset, it's crucial to monitor and moderate content to ensure quality and alignment with your brand values. Explore practical tips for implementing moderation processes, setting guidelines, and using user-generated content to enhance your brand narrative responsibly.

27.8 Measuring the Impact of UGC: Analytics and Insights

To gauge the success of your UGC efforts, delve into the world of analytics and insights. Learn how to measure the impact of user-generated content on key performance indicators (KPIs) and adjust your strategy accordingly. This chapter provides step-by-step guides on tracking UGC metrics, analyzing audience engagement, and refining your approach for optimal results.

Epilogue: Your User-Generated Content Mastery

As you conclude this exploration of user-generated content, recognize its potential to transform your social media strategy. Embrace the creativity of your community, encourage authentic contributions, and leverage UGC as a catalyst for brand growth. Your mastery of user-generated content will not only amplify your brand's reach but also foster a deeper connection with your audience. Happy cultivating!

Chapter 26: Unlocking the Wealth Potential of a Marketing Career

As you navigate the enchanting realms of marketing, it's worth exploring how a career in this dynamic field can be a pathway to financial prosperity. This chapter provides practical insights and strategies to unlock the wealth potential of a marketing career.

Understanding the Value of Marketing Skills

In the modern business landscape, marketing skills are highly valued. Whether you specialize in digital marketing, content creation, or data analytics, your expertise is in demand. Companies recognize the pivotal role marketing plays in reaching and resonating with their target audience. By continually honing your skills, staying abreast of industry trends, and adapting to new technologies, you position yourself as an invaluable asset.

Negotiating Your Worth

One of the keys to building wealth in a marketing career lies in your ability to negotiate your worth. As your skills and experience grow, don't be afraid to negotiate for competitive salaries and additional perks. Research industry standards, showcase your achievements, and confidently communicate the value you bring to the table. Negotiating effectively can significantly impact your earning potential and accelerate your journey to financial success.

Exploring Entrepreneurial Ventures

Many successful marketers have ventured into entrepreneurship, leveraging their skills to build their own businesses. Whether it's starting a consultancy, launching an e-commerce store, or creating a marketing agency, entrepreneurship offers the potential for substantial financial rewards. This chapter provides practical tips on identifying entrepreneurial opportunities, developing business plans, and navigating the challenges of starting your own venture.

Investing in Your Personal Brand

In the age of personal branding, marketing professionals have a unique advantage. By strategically building and promoting your personal brand, you can attract lucrative opportunities and partnerships. This chapter offers step-by-step guidance on crafting a compelling personal brand, leveraging social media platforms, and positioning yourself as an industry authority. A strong personal brand not only enhances your professional reputation but can open doors to lucrative collaborations and business ventures.

Maximizing Passive Income Streams

Beyond your primary role, exploring passive income streams can significantly contribute to your financial success. Whether it's writing a book, creating online courses, or investing in income-generating assets, this chapter provides actionable tips on diversifying your income. Learn how to leverage your marketing expertise to create valuable products or invest wisely, allowing your wealth to grow even when you're not actively working.

Epilogue: A Wealthy and Fulfilling Marketing Journey

Congratulations on unlocking the wealth potential of your marketing career! As you implement these strategies, remember that true wealth goes beyond monetary gains—it encompasses fulfillment, impact, and continuous growth. Stay curious, keep refining your skills, and embrace the ever-evolving nature of the marketing landscape. May your marketing journey not only make you financially rich but *also bring a sense of accomplishment and joy. Here's to a prosperous and fulfilling career in marketing!*

Conclusion: Your Journey to Marketing Mastery

As we draw the curtains on this comprehensive guide to marketing mastery, it's evident that the world of marketing is an ever-evolving landscape filled with opportunities, challenges, and endless possibilities. Throughout these chapters, we've explored the magical realms of marketing—from the fundamental principles to the cutting-edge trends that shape the industry.

Whether you're a seasoned marketer looking to refine your skills or a novice eager to embark on this captivating journey, the key takeaway is clear: mastery in marketing is a continuous process. It involves staying curious, adapting to change, and embracing the enchanting dance between creativity and strategy.

From the alchemy of crafting compelling content to the sorcery of data analytics, each facet of marketing holds its own magic. As you navigate the twists and turns of this dynamic landscape, remember that your journey is unique. Your brand's story, your audience, and your approach

to marketing all contribute to the tapestry of your success.

The practical tips, step-by-step guides, and insights into the latest trends are your tools on this journey. They are the wand you wield to cast spells of engagement, conversion, and brand loyalty. Yet, beyond the technical aspects, your passion, authenticity, and commitment to continuous learning are the true potions that fuel your success.

As you step into the future of marketing, may you do so with confidence, creativity, and an unwavering belief in the magic you bring to the table. Whether you find yourself negotiating lucrative deals, exploring entrepreneurial ventures, or crafting innovative campaigns, let your journey be both prosperous and fulfilling.

Remember that marketing, at its core, is about connecting with people, telling stories, and creating experiences that resonate. As you continue to refine your craft, may your marketing spells captivate hearts, inspire action, and leave an indelible mark on the world.

Wishing you a magical and fulfilling journey in the realms of marketing. May your brand shine brightly, your audience engage enthusiastically, and your career be a testament to the endless possibilities that marketing mastery brings. Happy spellcasting!

Good luck
the best marketer in the world.

www.ingramcontent.com/pod-product-compliance
Lightning Source LLC
Chambersburg PA
CBHW072229290526
45794CB00007B/2941